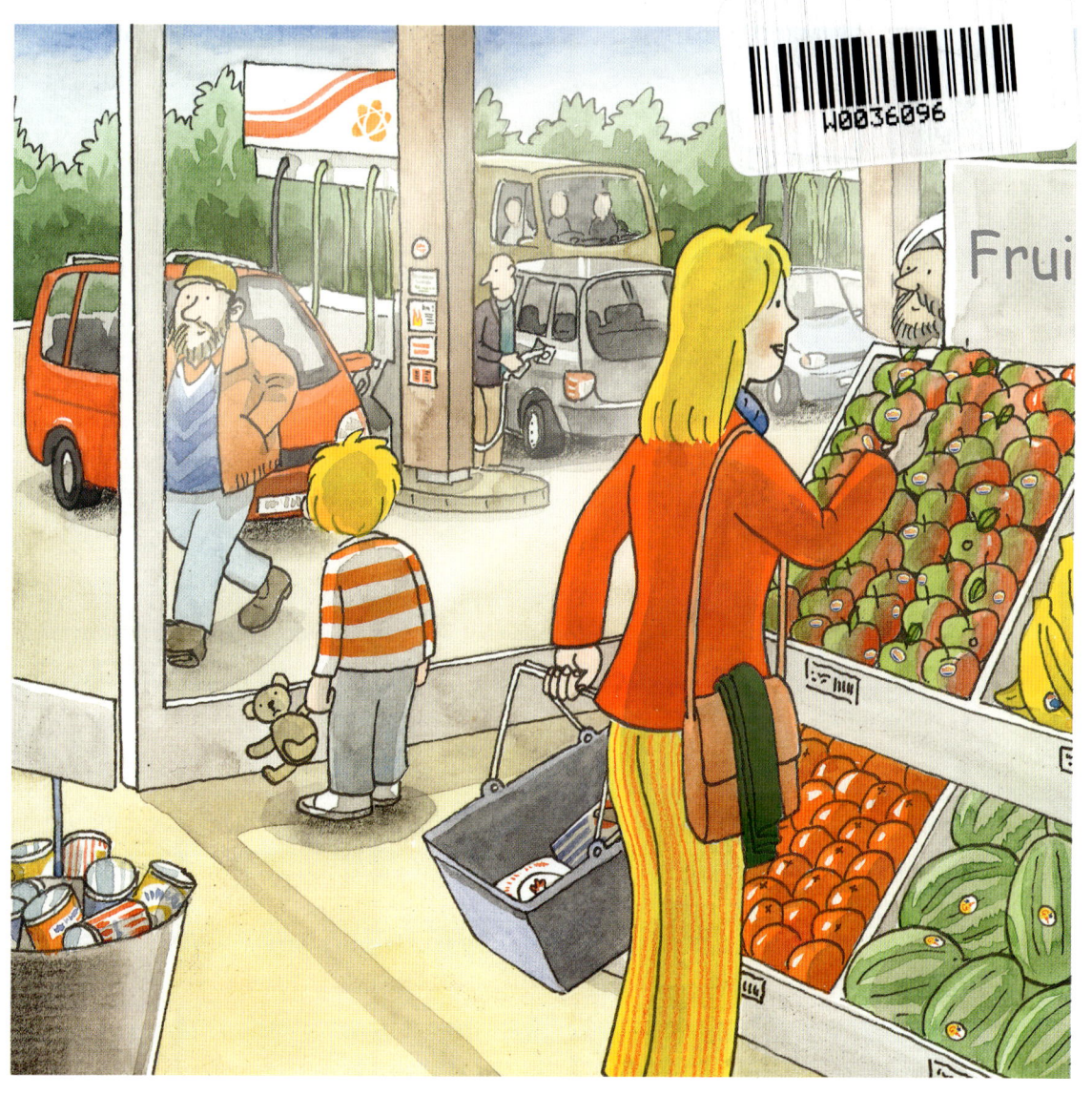

Mum got the shopping.

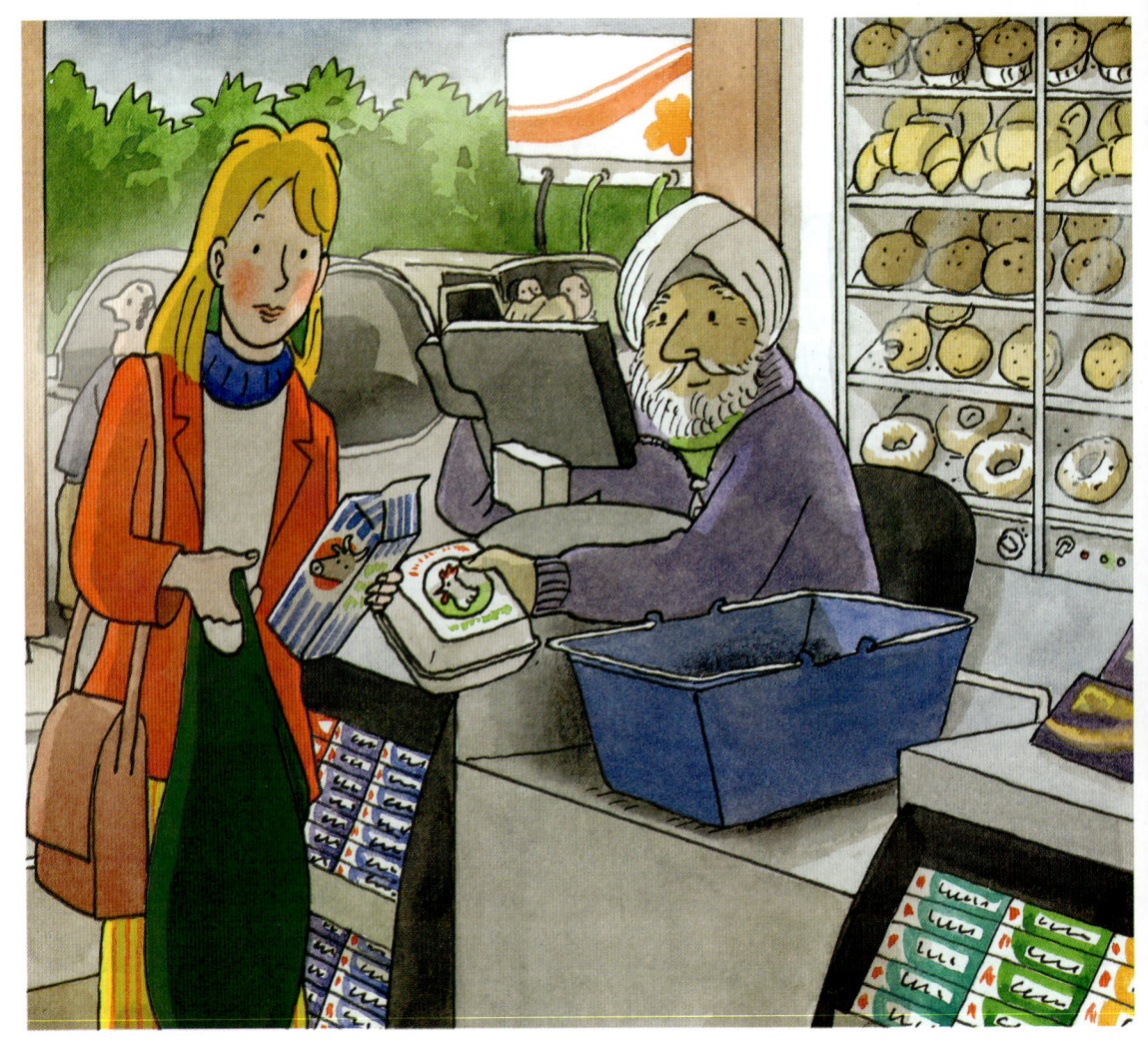

Mum put it in a bag.

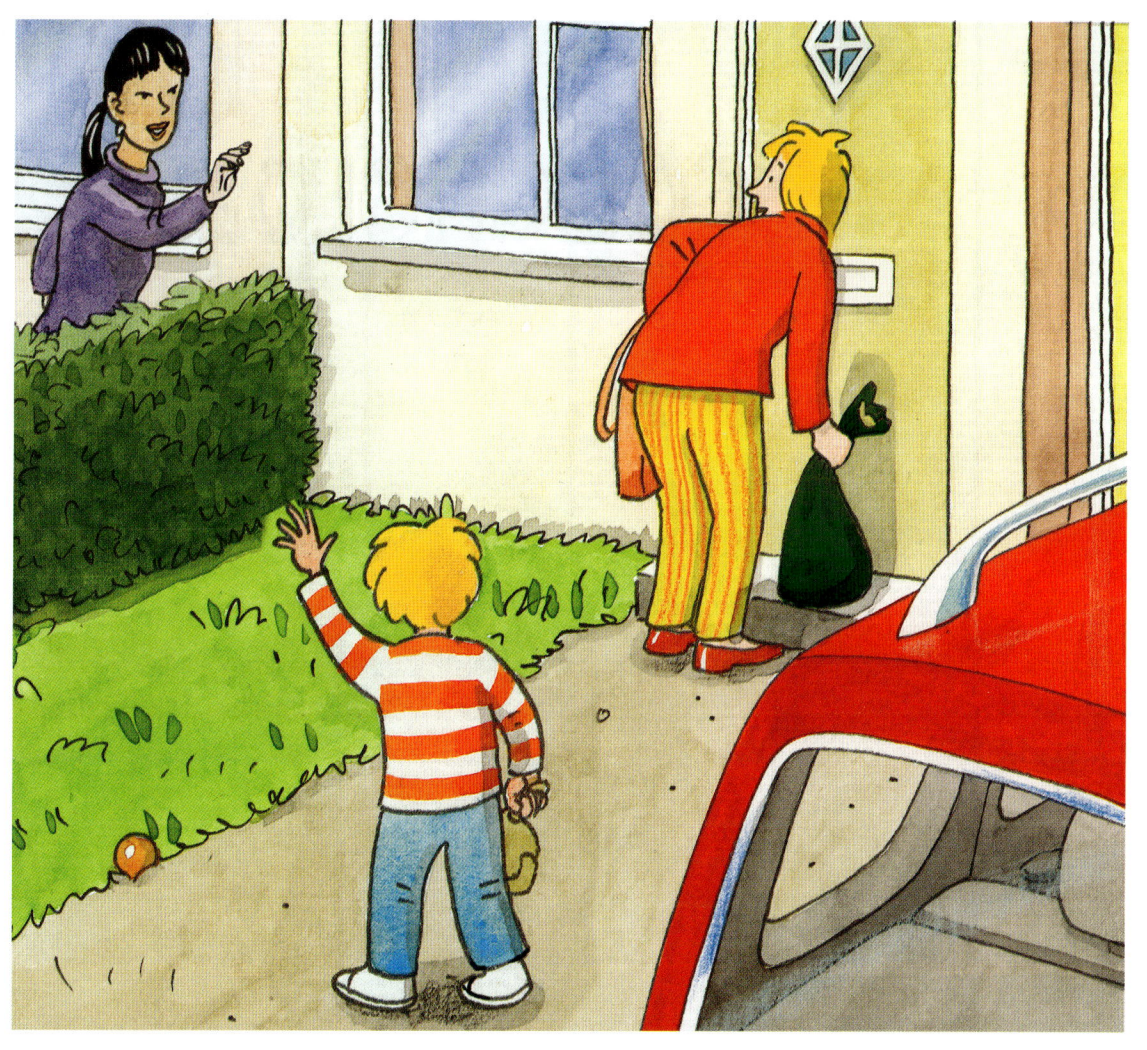

Mum put the bag on
the step.

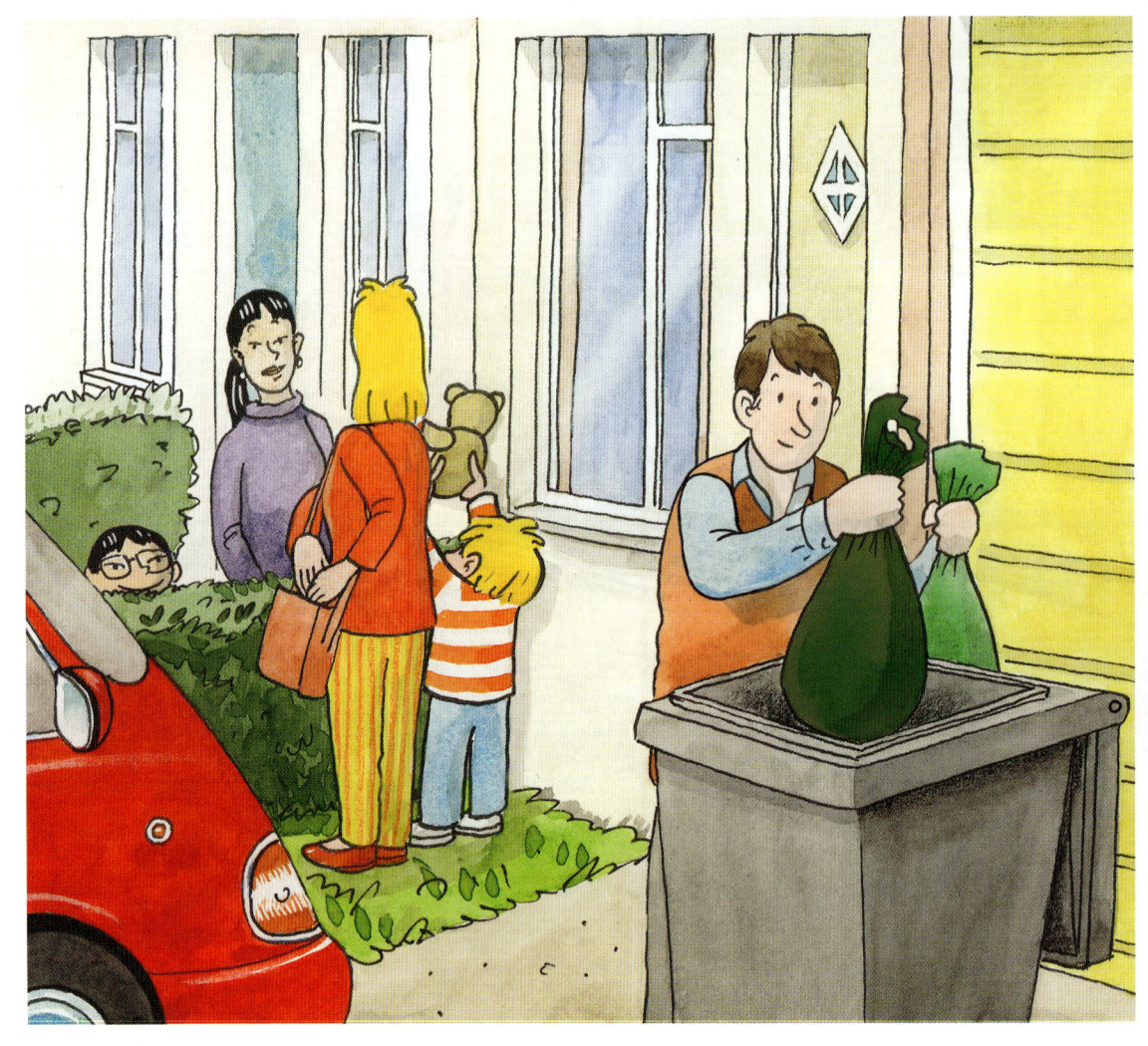

Dad put the shopping
in the bin.

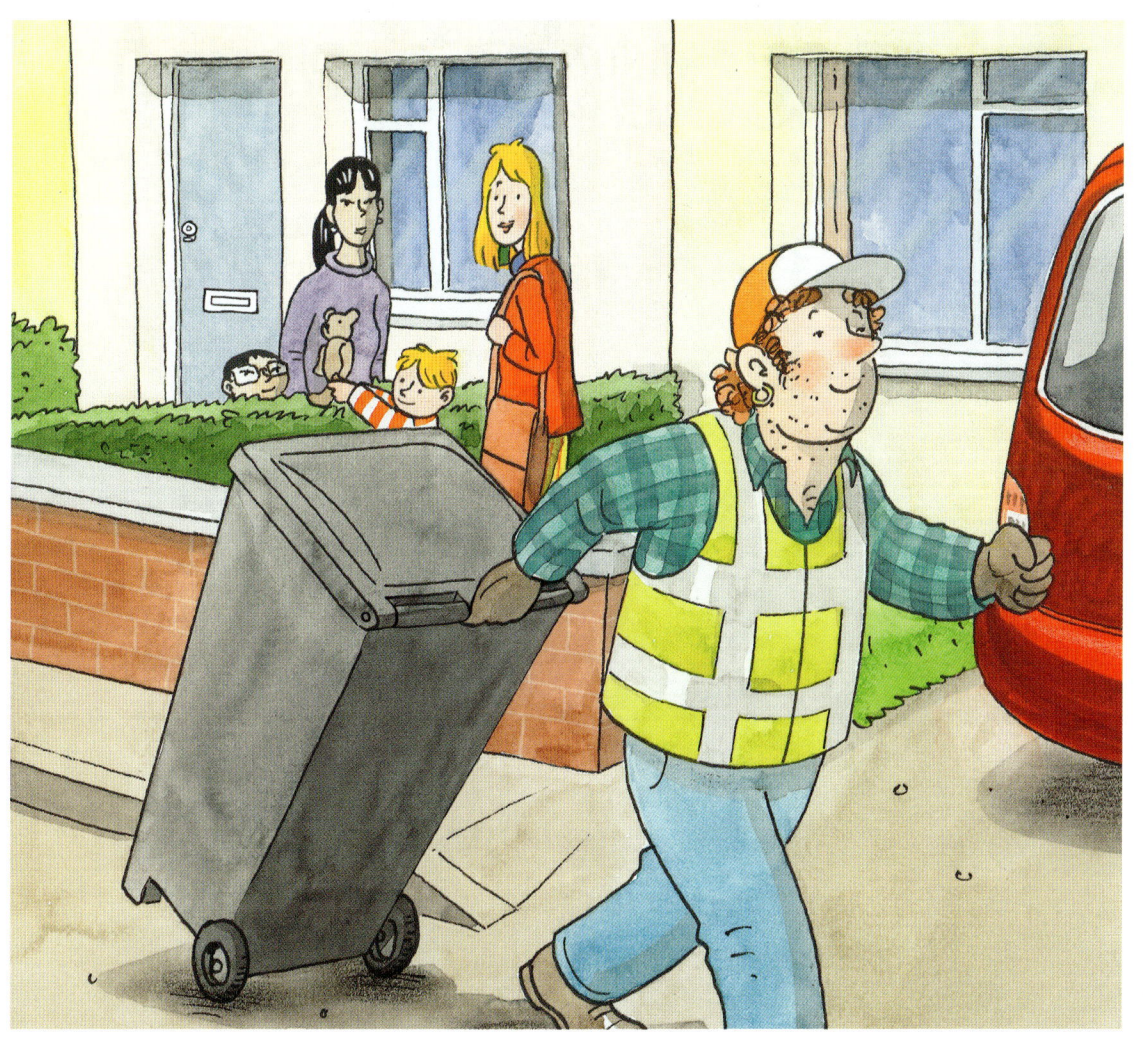

The bin man took the bin.

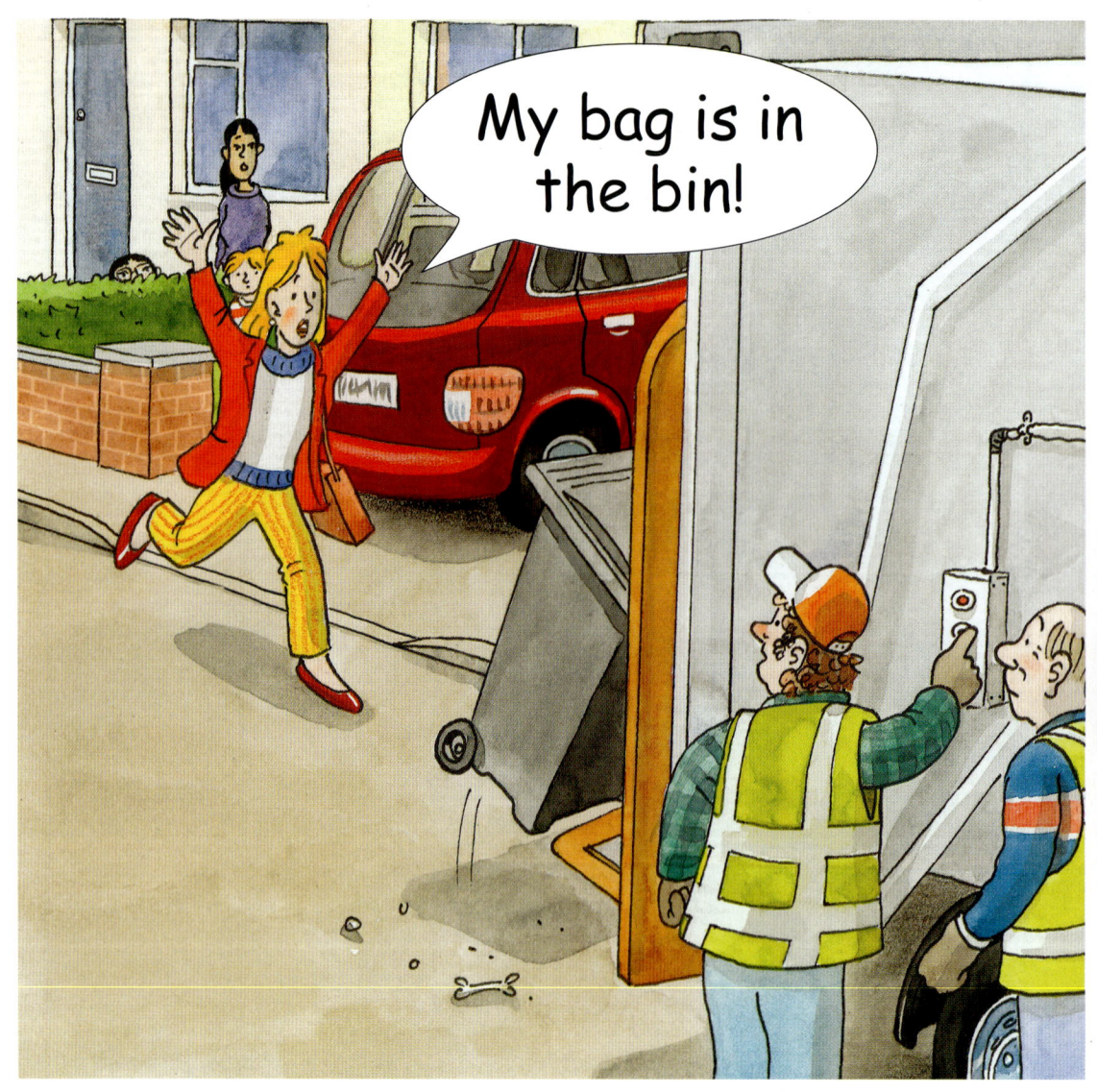

Mum ran to the bin men.

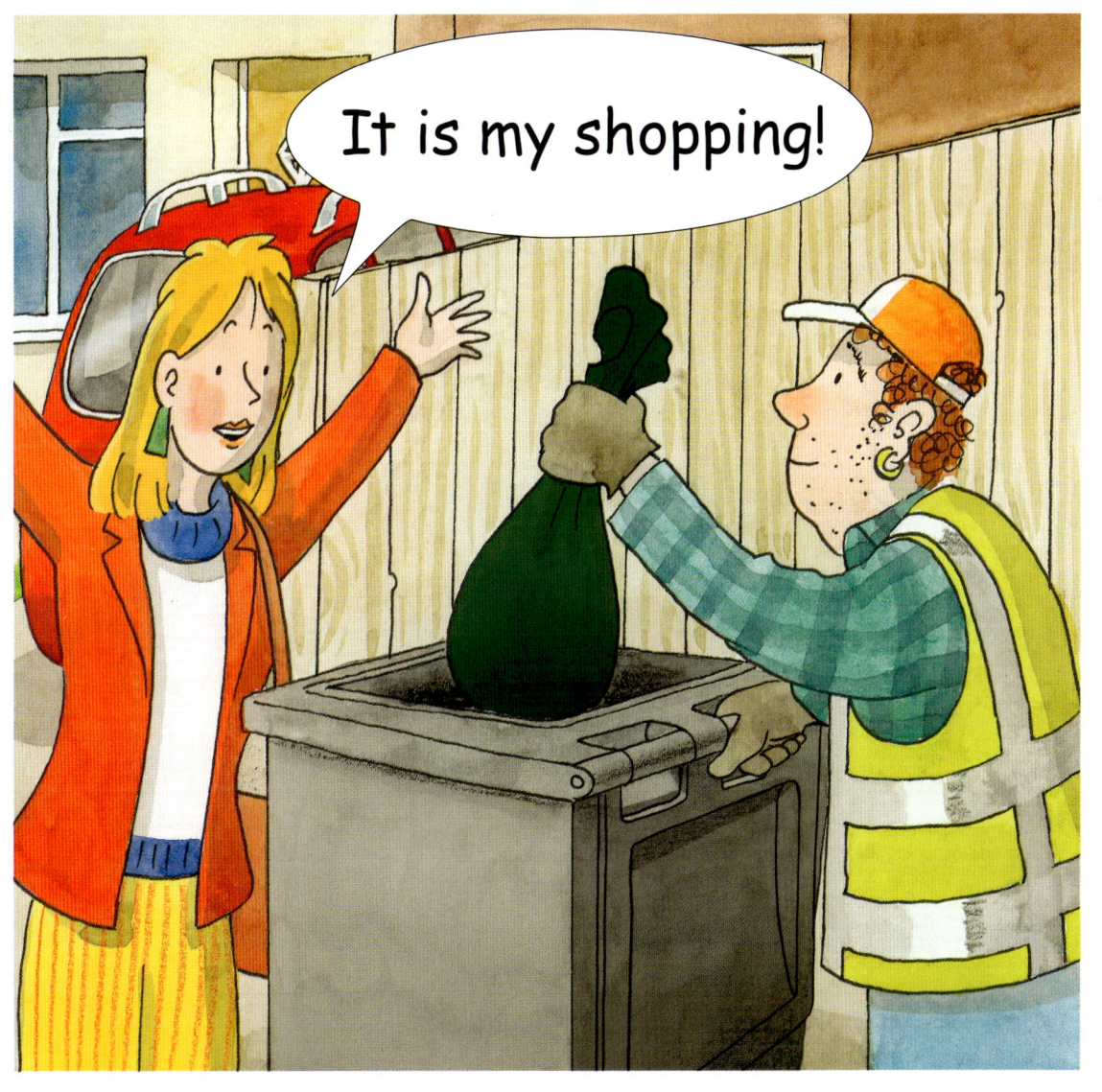

The bin man got the bag.

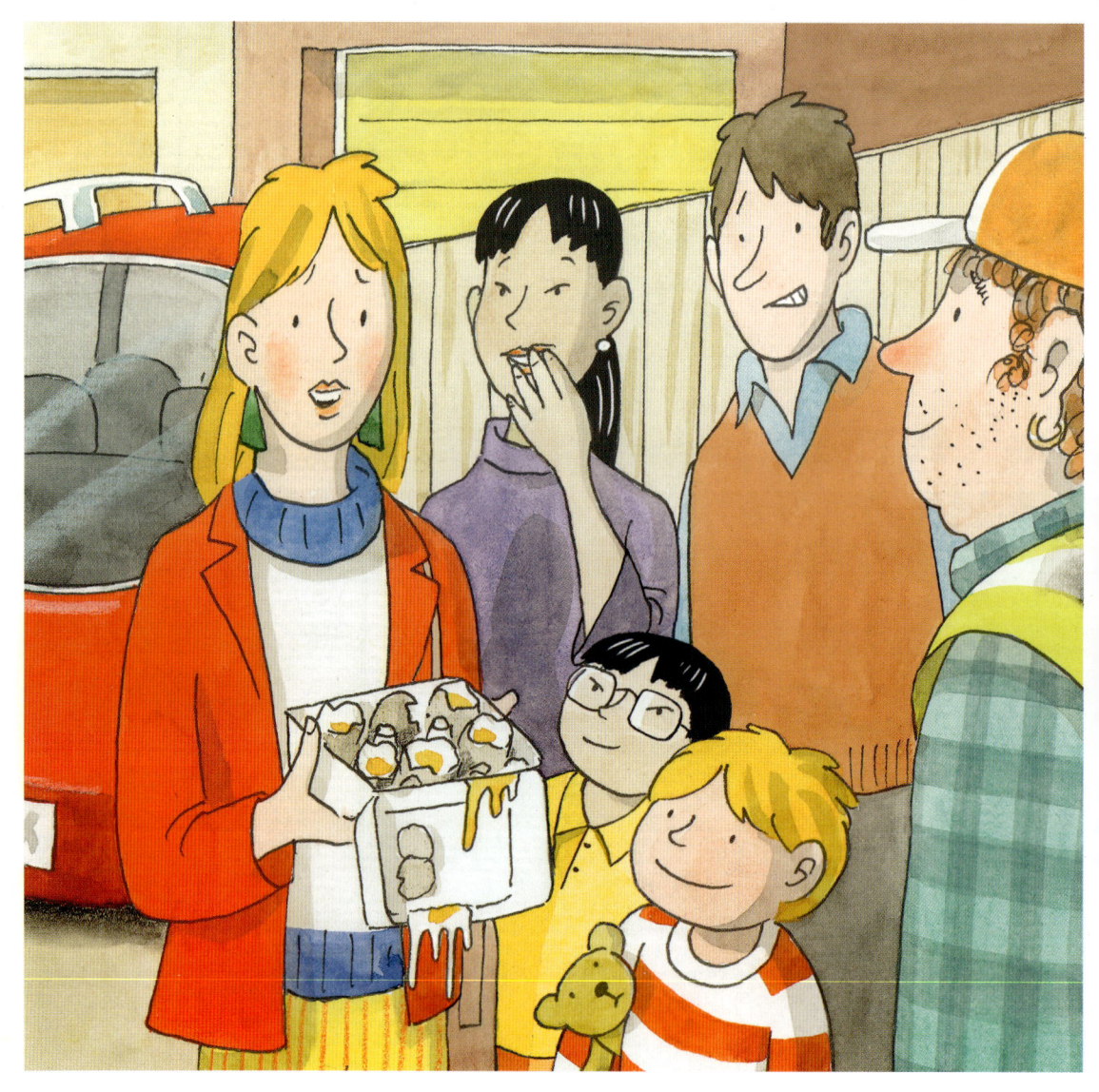

Oh no! Scrambled eggs.